Contents

The water cycle 4

How to make a rain gauge 6

Where is the world's water? 8

Too little or too much water 10

Water diary 1 12

Helping thirsty people 14

How to build a well 16

Is it a good idea? 18

Who uses water? 20

Moving water 22

How is water recycled? 24

Water diary 2 26

Save our water! 28

Who owns water? – I do! 30

Why was water a problem in Victorian towns and cities? 32

Why do people live by the River Nile? 34

How does a shaduf work? 36

How a river shapes the land 38

River research 40

River investigation 42

Glossary 44

Bibliography 46

Index 47

Thanks to the UK's mains water and sewerage system life-threatening water-related diseases are now very rare here. This is not true in many developing countries, where millions of people still have to drink dirty water. Clean water is essential for life and for health; it should be treasured.

The piece on Victorian towns and cities tells how the cholera epidemic showed the need for a clean water supply and sewers (p32). Let's hope this century will see the eradication of water-related diseases in developing countries too.

Libby Clarke
Communications Services Manager WaterAid

The water cycle

Water is a natural resource found nearly everywhere, both on the land and in the sky. It fills ponds, rivers, lakes and oceans. Constantly on the move, it falls as rain, flows from **springs**, runs in rivers and seeps deep underground.

The water cycle explains how and why water continuously moves in a circular pattern, moving from the sky to the land and back to the sky again. The cycle is complex because water changes state as it travels. With changes in temperature and air pressure, water can become a gas (water vapour), a liquid (rivers, lakes, rain) or a solid (hail, snow).

Tiny water droplets combine to form larger droplets.

Water falls back to land as rain or snow.

Some water flows underground.

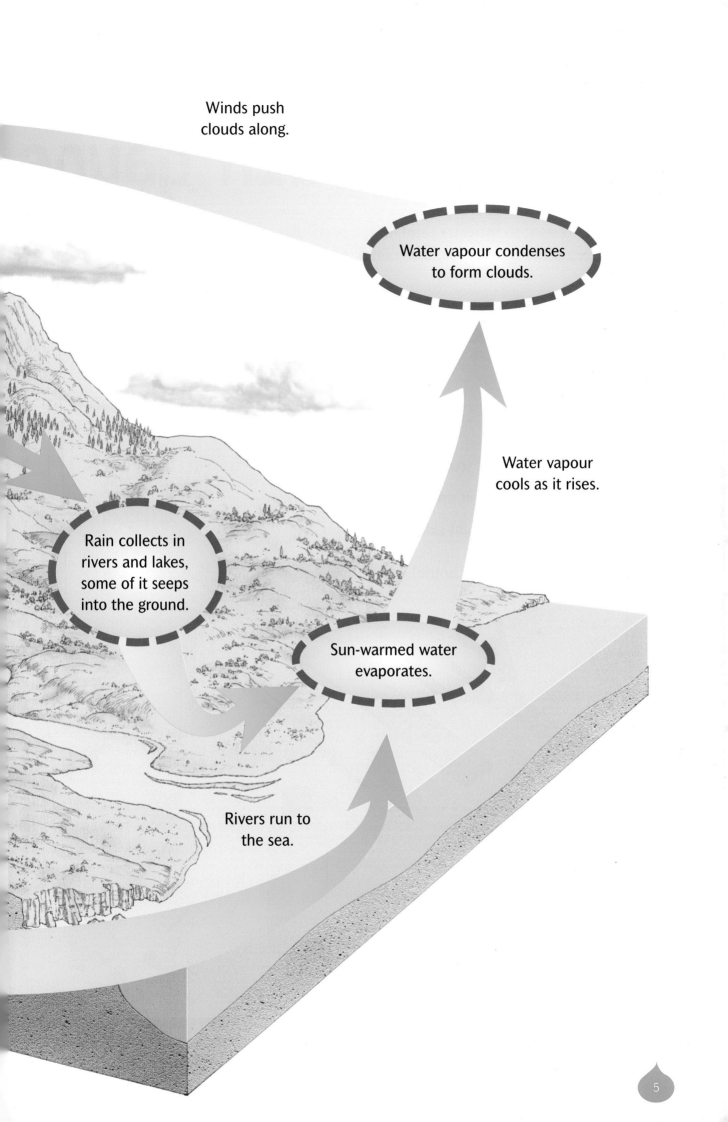

Winds push
clouds along.

Water vapour condenses
to form clouds.

Water vapour
cools as it rises.

Rain collects in
rivers and lakes,
some of it seeps
into the ground.

Sun-warmed water
evaporates.

Rivers run to
the sea.

How to make a rain gauge

A rain gauge is used to measure rainfall in a particular area, and to reproduce rainfall graphs like those on page 9.

You will need:

- sharp scissors
- waterproof pen
- ruler
- measuring jug with cc (cubic centimetre) scale
- 1.5 litre clear plastic soft drinks bottle
- 300–500 ml clear, straight-sided plastic bottle (e.g. empty bubble bath bottle)

Warning

Before using scissors always check with an adult first.

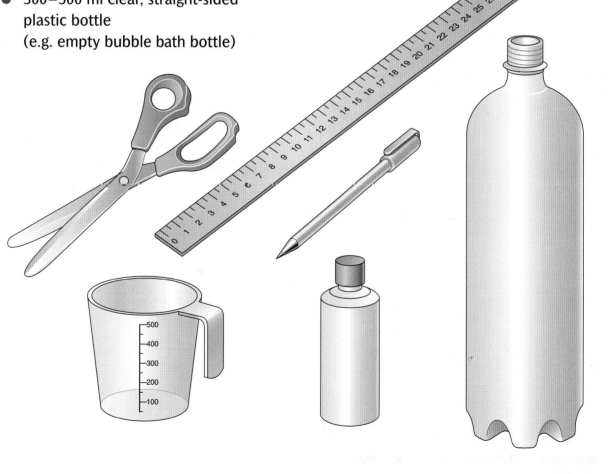

1 Discard the lids from both the bottles, then wash the bottles thoroughly.

2 Cut the top off the soft drinks bottle about 8 cm down from the neck of the bottle. Cut a straight edge all around.

3 Cut the top off the smaller plastic bottle. The cut should be below the bottle's neck.

4 Fill the measuring jug with 100 cc of water. Check the measure is accurate.

5 Pour the water into the smaller plastic bottle. Mark the water level on the side of the bottle with the waterproof pen.

6 Fill the bottle with another 100 cc measure and mark the next water level. Repeat several times to create a scale up the side of the bottle. Use the ruler to make sure the scale goes straight up one side of the bottle.

7 Pour the water out of the bottle. Next, place it upright in the bottom section of the soft drinks bottle.

8 Use the top of the drinks bottle and place upside down in the top of the smaller bottle to act as a funnel.

9 Place the rain gauge upright in a hole in the ground outside, so that the top of the funnel is 300 mm above ground level.

10 Check the water level in the bottle and record the readings every morning.

500 cc of water is equal to 1 cm of rain

Where is the world's

Almost all the world's water – about 98% of it – is in the oceans, but this water is too salty to use. The rest of the world's water is found in rivers, lakes, dams and under the ground, but three-quarters of it is trapped as ice in **glaciers** and in the **ice-caps** of the Arctic and Antarctica.

dry climate

However, this small percentage still amounts to a lot of **fresh water** being present on our planet, although water is not always available in some areas of the world. This is due to **climate** and weather. While some areas have wet climates, with plentiful rain all year round, others have dry climates and may suffer from frequent **droughts**.

The climate of an area depends on the average weather (temperature, rainfall, air pressure, wind, humidity, sunshine, etc.) over a number of years. An area's climate is affected by all kinds of factors, such as **latitude**, **altitude** and its position in relation to an ocean or mountain range.

Many towns and cities are alongside rivers which provide a constant source of water. Other sources include lakes, dams, **springs**, wells and **bore holes**. However, in some climates even these water sources may dry up during the dry season.

wet climate

water?

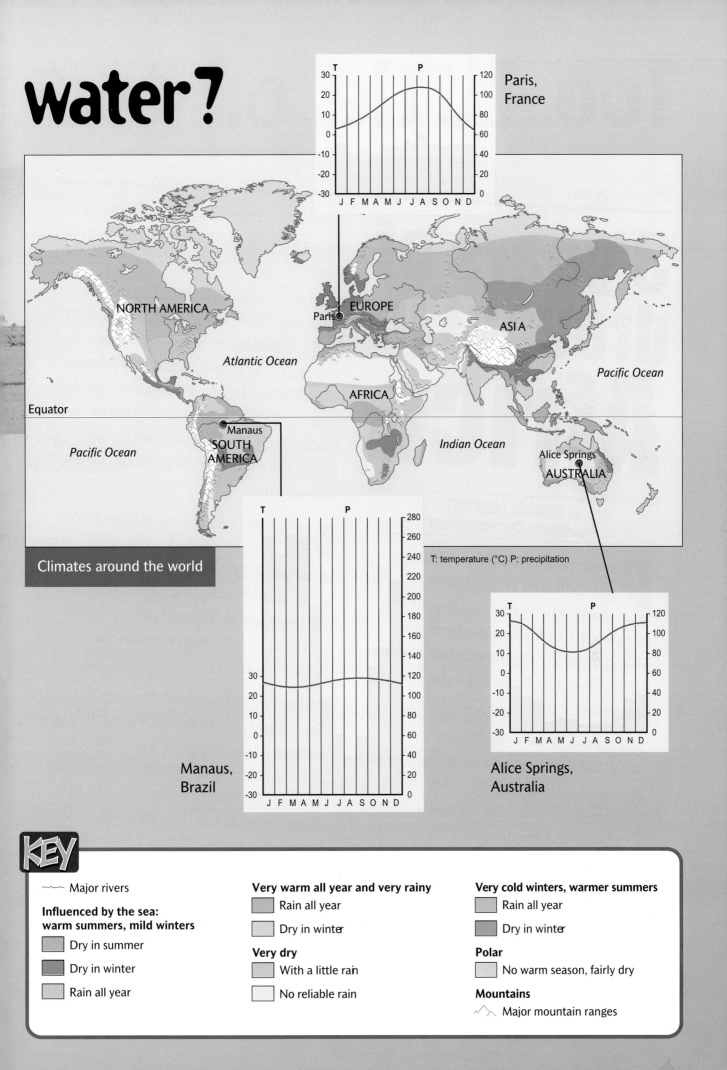

Paris, France

T: temperature (°C) P: precipitation

Climates around the world

NORTH AMERICA

EUROPE

Paris

ASIA

Atlantic Ocean

Pacific Ocean

Equator

Manaus

SOUTH AMERICA

AFRICA

Indian Ocean

Alice Springs

AUSTRALIA

Pacific Ocean

Manaus, Brazil

Alice Springs, Australia

KEY

~~~ Major rivers

**Influenced by the sea:
warm summers, mild winters**

☐ Dry in summer

☐ Dry in winter

☐ Rain all year

Very warm all year and very rainy

☐ Rain all year

☐ Dry in winter

Very dry

☐ With a little rain

☐ No reliable rain

Very cold winters, warmer summers

☐ Rain all year

☐ Dry in winter

Polar

☐ No warm season, fairly dry

Mountains

∧∧ Major mountain ranges

Too little or too

12 July 2000

3 years of drought in Africa

By REBECCA CRABTREE
Geography Correspondent

People in south-eastern Ethiopia are suffering from a third consecutive year of **drought**. An estimated 13 million people are affected. In the Ogaden District alone, 1.2 million people face the danger of starvation.

South-eastern Ethiopia has been described as a dust bowl. The lack of rain has turned the region into a hot, dry and **inhospitable** area. Plants cannot survive, so very few crops are being harvested. Grasses are drying up, leaving animals without pastureland.

Around 70% of the people in the region are nomadic, which means they travel around looking for **fresh water** and pasture for their livestock. However, in this drought-stricken area, both are almost non-existent, and so many animals have died. If any have survived, farmers have been forced to sell them to buy food.

Thousands of people have left the region to escape the dust and heat, and in search of aid. People who have nothing are waiting for help from local and national aid agencies. In one village, 3000 people have settled in a temporary **refugee camp**. They have nothing but their makeshift homes, built from cardboard or animal skins.

At one camp, one in ten children have died because of the lack of medicines to treat their hunger-related diseases. In some areas, food-aid stations have not yet been set up. Even in places where there are aid stations, supplies are running out.

Aid agencies have been begging for help for months. Since television has brought images of the suffering into people's homes, there have been many promises of help. However, it takes time to get supplies to where they are needed. Civil war in the region makes it difficult for aid agencies to operate safely. Bandits ambush trucks carrying supplies. One agency worker said, "It is a difficult task, but we have to get the aid to where it is needed quickly. For many, it is already too late."

much water

Flood victims
- 165 people missing
- Isolated villages
- People stranded on rooftops
- 208 people dead
- Orphans

Resources lost
- Food stores flooded
- Starvation
- Crops destroyed
- Animals killed

Heavy annual monsoon rains cause flooding in eastern India – September, 2000

Rescue/aid
- Local/international aid agencies called in
- Army rescuers in boats
- Helicopters drop food/water

Destruction
- Can lead to disease/dehydration
- Water supply damaged/contaminated
- 800,000 homes lost
- Cost more than £40 million

Transport networks
- Railway tracks washed away
- Roads flooded

Water diary 1

Christina's Diary

Hot/dry **climate**

Christina in Ghana, Africa

No rain for 8 months a year

No water supply in village

7 a.m. set off to water hole

Only supply of water for miles (no choice)

Journey

1 hour

8 a.m. arrived at water hole

Water not clean

Cattle watered

**9 a.m.
leave water hole**

10.15 a.m.

Pot of water
heavy

**11 a.m.
More water
used – drinking**

4 p.m.

Journey

Afternoon

1 hour 15 minutes

Remaining water
used – drinking

Carried pot
for whole
family

Half water
used up

Christina sets off
for more water

Villagers
wash clothes

**Noon
More water
used – washing**

Water used to
prepare food

Photographs taken from the WaterAid video *'Buckets of water'*

Helping thirsty people

While the majority of people in the UK can turn on a tap for a drink of water, to fill a bath or wash their car, over a billion people in the world do not have access to any clean water. Surely such inequality is unfair and unacceptable.

Unsafe **contaminated** water carries disease and, at present, a child dies from disease every 15 seconds because he or she does not have a supply of clean water. Many people have no choice but to drink dirty water.

People have many different needs around the world, but water is one of the common necessities for life. Surely it is time that everyone had a supply of clean water. It is essential for a healthy life – and is relatively cheap to supply. How can the water-rich continue to ignore those who are less fortunate?

The charity, WaterAid, has a 'vision of a world where everyone has access to safe water and effective sanitation'. It is essential to support such charities.

When there is a drought, crops wither and animals die. People are left without food and then face starvation. Starving people are especially vulnerable to the deadly diseases carried in contaminated water. Therefore, when there is such a crisis, a supply of clean water is vital. During a drought in the Sudan, in June 1998, the charity Oxfam set about drilling 22 wells and fitting pumps so that people did not have to drink contaminated surface waters*.

The above example of aid is one of many thousands. With financial aid, charities can try to get **fresh water** to anyone. Wells and pumps can be dug and supplied quite cheaply. For example, it costs just £10 to provide safe water for life for one person living in the developing world**.

* Oxfam and Water –
Clean water in emergencies
www.oxfam.org.uk

** What is WaterAid? –
leaflet produced by WaterAid

How to build a well

You will need:

- reinforced concrete rings
- gravel, sand, clay
- external concrete apron
- top slab
- hand pump

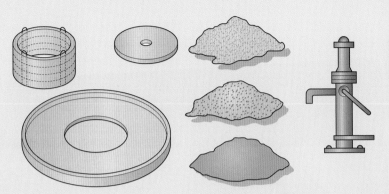

1 Digging

first concrete ring lowered

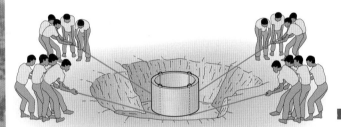

2 Deepening

SAFETY NOTICE

Workers should always wear helmets

3 Adding rings

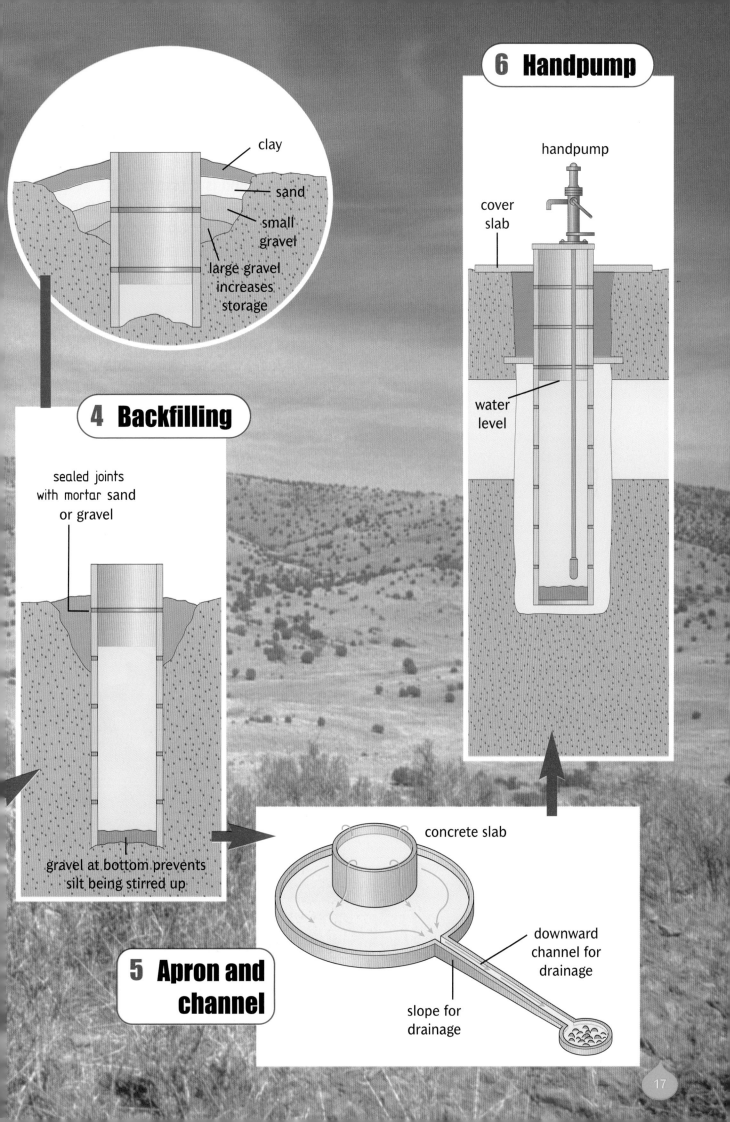

clay

sand

small
gravel

large gravel
increases
storage

4 Backfilling

sealed joints
with mortar sand
or gravel

gravel at bottom prevents
silt being stirred up

6 Handpump

handpump

cover
slab

water
level

concrete slab

downward
channel for
drainage

slope for
drainage

**5 Apron and
channel**

Is it a good idea?

The Three Gorges Dam in China is a prestigious project for China. As the largest **hydroelectric** dam in the world, it will be a brilliant feat of engineering.

Inevitably, the costs are high – but not that great for 'a dream for generations to come'. That's what China's American embassy called it.

In 1991, floodwaters from the Yangtze affected 200 million people and caused the deaths of nearly 2000. The dam will prevent flooding and save lives.

Benefits

◆ 84.7bn kw/h of power supplied

◆ clean energy will not create any pollution

◆ reliable source of water

◆ better **navigation** along the Yangtze River

◆ **irrigation** improved

The project is a waste of money, costing nearly US$29 billion. It will cause far greater damage than good.

The costs will be high on the environment, wildlife and the people of the area will be flooded by the lake behind the dam.

Some engineers think the way the dam is to be constructed will lead to a build up of sediment. This could make the dam less effective.

Problems

- **reservoir** (lake behind the dam) will be 600 kilometres in length
- wildlife will be destroyed, ecosystems will be disrupted
- 1000-year-old buildings will be destroyed by explosives or flooded
- the dam will flood 1000 people's homes
- people forced to resettle on poor-quality land

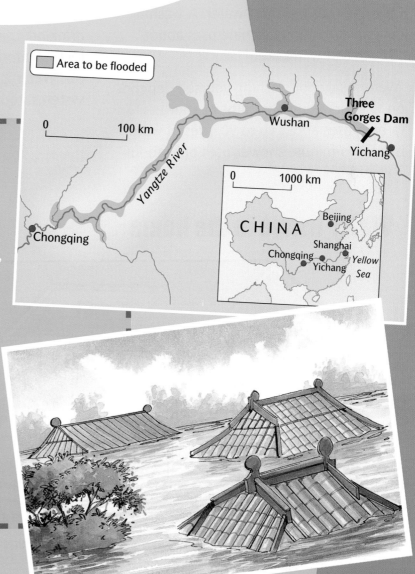

Area to be flooded

0   100 km

Yangtze River

Wushan

Three Gorges Dam

Yichang

0   1000 km

CHINA

Beijing

Shanghai

Chongqing

Chongqing

Yichang

Yellow Sea

Who uses water?

Water is essential for all life. Without it human beings, animals and plants die. The average human body is approximately 70-75% water. As water is lost all the time in the body, it has to be replaced by the water found in drinks and food. However, this is not the only way in which water is directly used by human beings. Houses, schools, hospitals and businesses require a constant source of water in their kitchens and bathrooms for cooking and personal hygiene, and to remove the **sewage** from toilets. Many factories use huge amounts of water in industrial processes.

HOMES

The average urban household (4.6 people) uses 640 litres of water per day at home*. Cleaning uses the most water. A washing cycle in a washing machine uses about 120 litres of water.

Water usage for washing yourself depends on whether you have baths or showers (a bath uses about 80 to 90 litres of water but a two-minute shower uses only about 20 litres). Other ways in which householders use water include flushing toilets, cleaning the house, cooking and drinking, carrying waste away, cleaning teeth, watering plants and washing the car. Water is often used in heating systems, too.

*(*source: www.thewaterpage.com)*

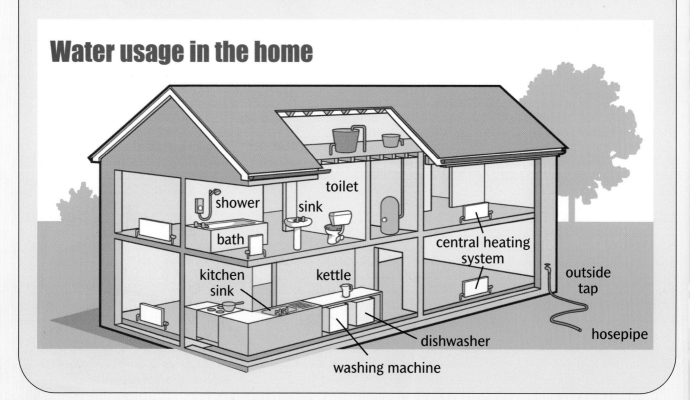

Water usage in the home

shower · sink · toilet · bath · central heating system · kitchen sink · kettle · outside tap · dishwasher · washing machine · hosepipe

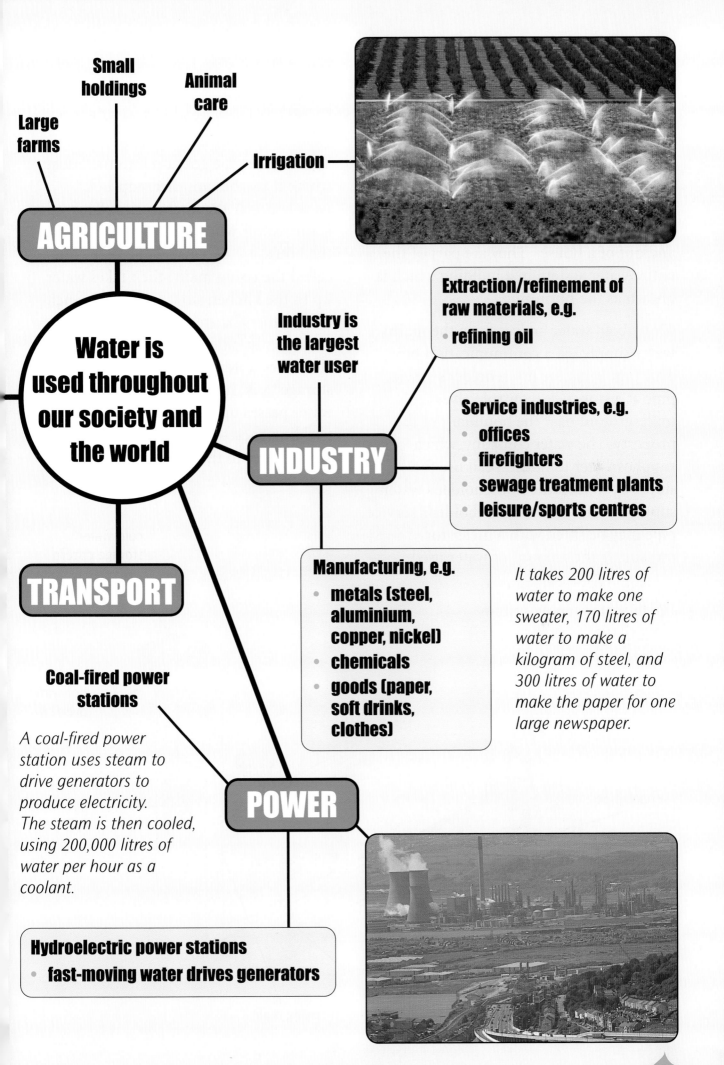

Small holdings

Large farms

Animal care

Irrigation

AGRICULTURE

Water is used throughout our society and the world

Industry is the largest water user

Extraction/refinement of raw materials, e.g.
- refining oil

INDUSTRY

Service industries, e.g.
- offices
- firefighters
- sewage treatment plants
- leisure/sports centres

TRANSPORT

Manufacturing, e.g.
- metals (steel, aluminium, copper, nickel)
- chemicals
- goods (paper, soft drinks, clothes)

It takes 200 litres of water to make one sweater, 170 litres of water to make a kilogram of steel, and 300 litres of water to make the paper for one large newspaper.

Coal-fired power stations

A coal-fired power station uses steam to drive generators to produce electricity. The steam is then cooled, using 200,000 litres of water per hour as a coolant.

POWER

Hydroelectric power stations
- **fast-moving water drives generators**

Moving water

In a house, there are many water pipes through which water flows. The pipes, tanks and controls, such as valves, allow for the safe passage of water in, around and out of a house. They are part of the entire water system in a building which is known as the **plumbing**.

Clean, cold water arrives from the **mains water** supply via a communication pipe. This pipe joins the householder's service pipe at a stopcock (control valve) underground near the boundary of the property. The water company, which supplies water to houses, can use the stopcock to turn the householder's water supply on or off. The householder's service pipe may be fitted with a meter for measuring the amount of water used.

The service pipe goes up into the house where it reaches another stopcock, usually under the kitchen sink. This valve is turned off when plumbing repairs in the house are necessary. The pipe (often called the rising main) then takes water up to the kitchen sink, and may branch off to other fixtures such as a washing machine. In older houses, the rising main also takes water up to a cold-water storage tank, high up in the house. The water passes up vertically – without trickling back – because of the pressure of the water in the mains.

Basic water supply system

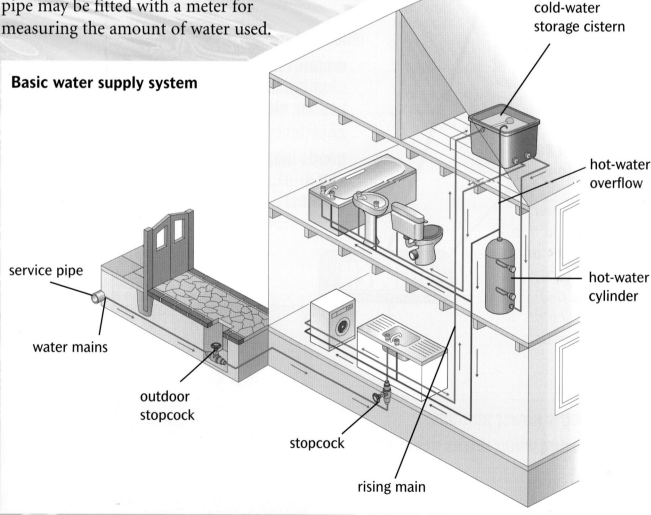

service pipe

water mains

outdoor stopcock

stopcock

rising main

cold-water storage cistern

hot-water overflow

hot-water cylinder

From the tank, the cold water travels down to other water outlets and appliances, such as taps, showers, toilet cisterns and water-heating systems. Water is usually heated in a boiler, stored in a cylinder and then piped to hot-water taps or other appliances. In newer houses, where there are no tanks, the water rises direct from the main which is permanently under pressure.

While the supply system of pipes brings clean water into a house, another system takes waste and dirty water away. This drainage system consists of larger pipes that lead to a single 'soil-and-waste' stack. This wide, vertical pipe drains all the waste water and solids to underground drains.

The drains usually lead to a water company's **sewer**, which takes the waste to a **sewage** works for treatment.

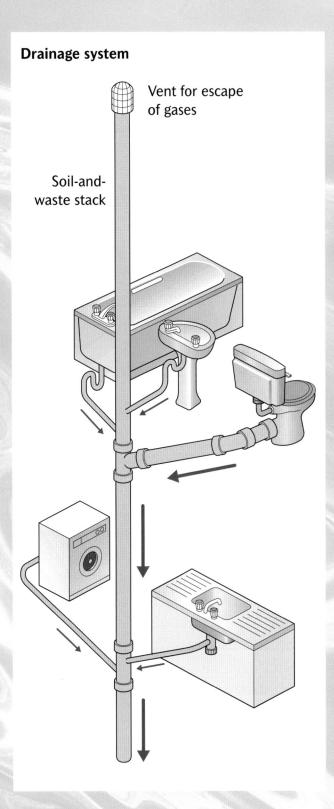

Drainage system

Vent for escape of gases

Soil-and-waste stack

How is water recycled?

Untreated water

This water may contain:

- poisonous chemicals from factories/farms
- diluted acids from industrial gases
- wild animal wastes
- disease-causing bacteria
- litter/rubbish
- twigs, leaves, dead animal remains
- particles of soil, grit, sand

WARNING: Untreated water is NOT safe to drink.

Rainwater collects in reservoirs and rivers or seeps underground into aquifers.

Water purification process

Before the water from **reservoirs** and rivers is pumped to houses, it is treated and purified at a waterworks. The purification process is necessary because unpurified **fresh water** can be a danger to health if consumed. Purification involves several stages. First, the water goes through a strainer (wire mesh) in order to filter out large objects, such as litter and leaves. Next, the water rests for a while in a settling tank so that smaller particles of dirt settle to the bottom. The clearer water above the settled particles is then passed through a filter bed. This is made up of a layer of sand and grit, which filters out any remaining dirt; and also organisms, which destroy some disease-carrying bacteria. Finally, chlorine (a gas) is passed through the water in order to destroy any dangerous organisms that may still be present.

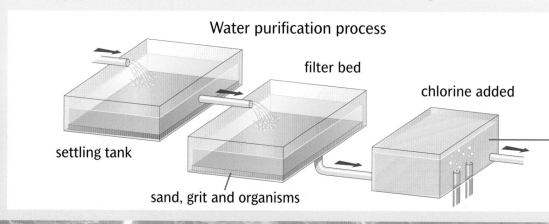

Water purification process

settling tank

filter bed

sand, grit and organisms

chlorine added

Returned to the natural water cycle

Sea/river water evaporates

Clean water pumped into sea or river

Waste water treated at sewage works

Sewage treatment by-products:
- methane gas (used as fuel to drive sewage work pumps)
- solid waste (used as a **fertilizer** on farms)

Purified water stored in tank/enclosed reservoir

Purified water is safe to drink.

Piped to houses/ schools/factories

Used, waste water is piped to **sewers** and drains.

Fluoride

Fluoride (to help prevent tooth decay) may be added.

Water diary 2

This extract was taken from Toby's diary. Toby has been keeping
a water diary for four days. He lives in Manchester.

After lunch I washed up for Mum. There wasn't much to wash so
we didn't use the dishwasher. I had to fill the washing-up bowl twice,
once to wash and once to rinse. I measured 14 half-litre jugfuls of
water in the bowl each time.

Afterwards, Mum set the washing machine going. Mum said
that nearly half the clothes in that load were mine, so I was
responsible for half the water the washing machine used!

I went to the toilet twice during the afternoon and washed my
hands afterwards. To wash my hands I used the half-litre jug to put
water in the handbasin. I used two jugfuls both times.

When Dad got back from his work at the shop, we washed the car.
It took seven buckets of water. I didn't use the hosepipe because it
would have been too difficult to measure how much water we used.

When we went inside I had some juice mixed with 200 ml of tap
water. Next I had a very quick shower before tea. I was only under the
shower for about one minute because I was in a rush but keeping the
water diary made me realize how often I spend quite a while in there!

At five o'clock, I helped make my own tea because I wanted to see
how much water would be used. First I washed some potatoes in about
one litre of water. Then Mum made some chips with them while I
poured nearly a litre of water in a saucepan to warm up
frankfurters. I drank a glass of fizzy water (300 millilitres) with
my meal. Dad used the dishwasher to wash up afterwards.

Apart from a glass of milk at bedtime, I didn't drink anything
else. I went to the toilet and washed my hands and face (1 litre).
I forgot to be careful with water and left the tap running when I
brushed my teeth. In bed I wrote this diary entry, using the notes
I had been keeping all day.

Approximate water usage

Drinking and cooking
(one person in a day): 25–30 litres

Washing machine: 120 litres

Dishwasher: 30 litres

Washing dishes
by hand: 14 litres

Bath: 80 litres

Shower: 10 litres a minute

Flushing a toilet: 10 litres

Brushing teeth with
tap running: 8–9 litres a minute

Save our water!

Friends of the Earth is an organization which campaigns to protect the environment. The following extracts were taken from their *Water Pollution* leaflet.

Clean water is essential for life. Every day each of us uses about 140 litres of water in our homes – over one full bath! But it is being polluted. Our rivers and underground water supplies are threatened by poisons leaking from waste dumps, chemicals from industry, and pollution from farms, while **sewage** pollutes some of our best beaches.

Wildlife is most at risk from this pollution. But some **pollutants** can make their way into our drinking water supply, potentially damaging our health.

What causes water pollution?

Factories **discharge** a wide range of toxic chemicals into rivers.

Ulcerated wounds on a fish caused by pollution

Modern farming methods use large amounts of **artificial fertilizers** and **pesticides**. Some of these chemicals leak into **groundwater** and rivers.

The **effluent** from sewage treatment works is probably the biggest polluter of the rivers.

Research published by Friends of the Earth in 1997 revealed that legal limits on water pollution were broken around two thousand times over a 12-month period.

Each household in the UK produces about one tonne of waste each year. Most of this ends up buried in **landfill sites**. When rubbish rots, harmful liquids can leak out and pollute groundwater supplies.

In some areas of England, human demand for water is draining our rivers dry.

Over 250 of our most important wildlife sites are under threat either because of declining availability of water or because of water pollution.

Finding out who is to blame!

If you are concerned that your drinking water might not meet all the [legal] standards, you can find out from your water company. Water companies do thousands of tests each year and the results are put on a public register kept by the company. You can visit your company's offices and look at the public register or write asking for information.

Take Action

- Save water – taking too much water from rivers reduces flow and concentrates pollution. Saving water also helps take pressure off important wildlife sites.

- Don't pour used oil or paint down the drain.

- Buy organic food and don't use polluting pesticides in your garden.

- Reduce waste – less rubbish in landfills means less groundwater pollution.

- Get pollution-spotting: report any water pollution you see to the Environment Agency. Their hotline number is 0800 807060.

- If your water company breaks the law, complain to the water company.

- If you don't think your water company is doing enough to stop pollution and water wastage, write to your own branch of the official regulator, OFWAT.

Who owns water?

14 Totts Road
Coltersbridge
Westshire
WS9 7TR

29th March 2002

Dear Sir/Madam

I am writing to complain about this year's water bill.
I cannot believe how absurdly high it is. In fact, I don't
understand why we have to pay for water at all!

Water comes naturally from the sky. You don't own it! I can
use rainwater that collects in my **water butt** for free, so
why can't I have a little of the water that falls in a
local lake? Why should you charge for something that nature
provides freely to everyone? After all, we don't have to
pay a company for the air we breathe!

It has rained and rained this winter. There must be plenty of
water around now, yet you are charging even more for it. This
is clearly unfair, unjust and unacceptable.

Certainly, we have to pay for pipes to be laid and to
maintain them, but ever-increasing charges for a plentiful,
natural **resource** that belongs to everyone cannot be tolerated.

Please review my bill (copy enclosed).

Yours faithfully

Jake Spencer

– I do!

Trimline Water Company

Coltersbridge   Henborough   Bernshire   2TT

Mr Jake Spencer
14 Totts Road
Coltersbridge
Westshire
WS9 7TR

5 April 2002

Dear Mr Spencer

I was sorry to receive your letter of complaint, as we are committed to providing our customers with an excellent service at a reasonable price.

Yes, water is a natural resource, but rainwater cannot be used in the home without being treated first. You can safely water your garden with it, but you cannot drink it and you cannot cook with it. If you did, you would be seriously endangering your health.

Trimline does not pretend to own rain. However, charges are made for the treatment and purification of water. Trimline constructs, maintains and operates treatment centres, purification processes, storage facilities and pipeline networks. Without these, you would not have a constant, reliable supply of clean, safe water.

I am sure you haven t forgotten that part of your water bill also covers the cost of removing and treating your waste water and **sewage**. You could treat these in your own home or garden of course, but you would require expensive equipment and a septic tank.

Water may fill the local lake today, but it could run dry tomorrow. Scientific reports tell us that, without doubt, temperatures in the UK will go up, possibly leading to terrible **droughts** in the future. Trimline is spending more money on water storage so that if there is a summer of searing heat, cool water will still run from your tap.

I am sorry I cannot revise your bill, but I am sure in view of the above you will see that we are fulfilling our commitment towards providing water and sewage treatment services at a reasonable price.

Yours sincerely

Margaret Headley
Manager

Why was water a problem in

Overcrowded housing

Steam-driven machines

Lots of factories built

Industrial Revolution

Growth of transport

People moved to towns/cities

In 1750 one fifth of the population lived in the cities

In 1850 half of the population lived in the cities

Increased water demands

Population of Britain grew from 500,000 in 1750 to 21 million in 1851

Increased waste

Main water sources

- rivers
- wells
- pumps

Limited access to water for washing away sewage

Limited water supplies

Few homes with inside tap so outside pumps used

Limited access to water for cleaning

No pure water supplies to homes

Victorian towns and cities?

Sewage seeped into ground

Sewage dumped into rivers

Diarrhoea

Open drains take away surface sewage only

Water contaminated

Typhoid

Cesspits not emptied

Poor sewage systems

Water problems – Victorian towns/cities (in 1850s)

Cholera

Extract from General Board of Health's Report 1850, description of Christopher Court, Rosemary Lane, London:

The court is a cul-de-sac … at the upper end is a large dust hole, full of filth of every description … on the first floor of one house, eight cases of cholera, of which three were fatal; the door at the foot of the stairs was shut, and on opening it I was repeatedly driven back by the horrid odour and stench of a privy downstairs… After getting upstairs my head reeked in the sickening atmosphere, and on reaching the top, and surrounded by the dead and dying, I was compelled to rush to the window and open it. I threw off the contents of my stomach, and supported myself on the miserable, rotten straw bed.

Later improvements

Public Health Act 1875

Town councils had to build effective **sewers** and provide clean water supply

1890: 95% London homes supplied with water

Why do people live

The River Nile, in Northeast Africa, is the longest river in the world (6,671 km). It flows through swampland, farmland and deserts, and past towns and villages. Lots of people live beside the River Nile for many different reasons.

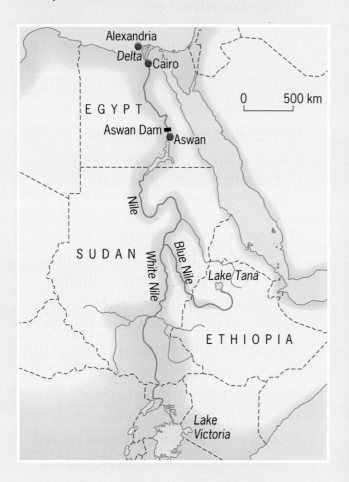

Water for growth

The Nile is an important source of water in the hot climate and desert regions of Egypt and the Sudan. Nearly all Egyptian farmers live beside the Nile or in the delta, using the water to irrigate their crops. The soil either side of the Nile is very fertile, so crops grow well. Village farmers grow crops to feed themselves and their families. Larger landowners encourage people to live beside the Nile by offering them work on their **commercial farms**.

Nomadic farmers from neighbouring desert regions come to the Nile so that their animals can drink and graze on the grassy river banks.

Employees working on sugar farms – in Egypt sugar is an important commercial crop.

Power for industry

The water of the Nile is used to generate power at the Aswan High Dam in Egypt and at other dams throughout its course. The electricity in turn has encouraged industries to develop near the river. Employees, such as mill workers and cotton factory workers, live nearby.

by the River Nile?

Settlements

The fertile soils and waters of the Nile have encouraged cities, towns and villages to develop along its banks since ancient times. The ruins of ancient Egyptian settlements bring many tourists (and people who work in tourism) to the river every year. The city of Cairo has developed on both sides of the river, and many different people live here today, drawn to the place for work, trade or education and to enjoy the many facilities such a city offers.

Some people live by the Nile because of the fishing industry.

Transport

Most of the Nile in Egypt and the Sudan is navigable and many people who work with river transport live beside the Nile. They may run ferries, river cruisers for tourists, or boats for transporting goods. Many people work in the river port of Alexandria.

How does a shaduf work?

Water is essential for the growth of plants. Farmers use
irrigation to add water to their crops, often in areas
where there is little rainfall. The shaduf has been used for
three thousand years in Egypt, to raise water from the
River Nile, in order to irrigate crops growing nearby.

A shaduf in use today

The shaduf

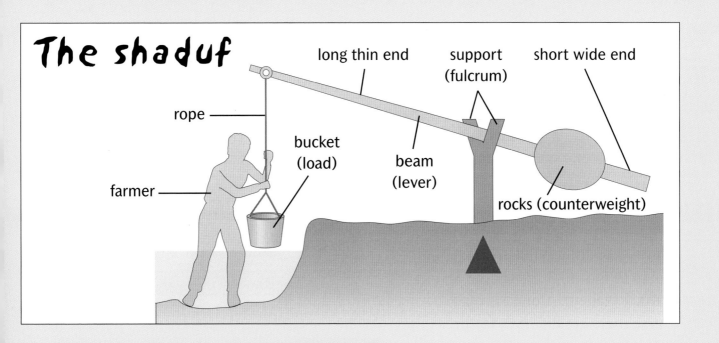

long thin end

support (fulcrum)

short wide end

rope

bucket (load)

farmer

beam (lever)

rocks (counterweight)

Lowering the bucket

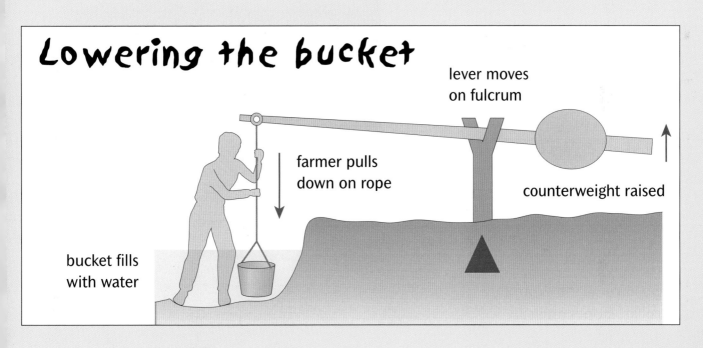

lever moves on fulcrum

farmer pulls down on rope

counterweight raised

bucket fills with water

Raising the bucket

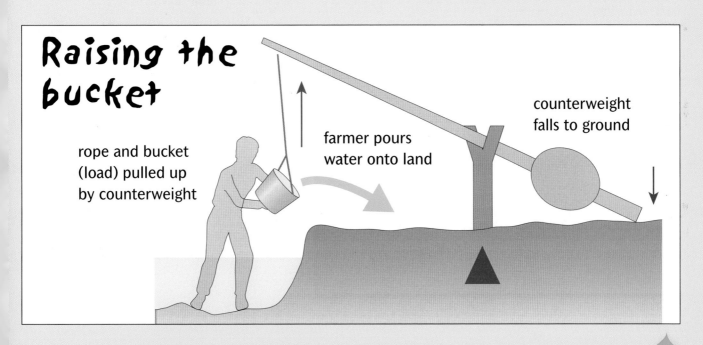

counterweight falls to ground

rope and bucket (load) pulled up by counterweight

farmer pours water onto land

How a river shapes the land

The start of a river is called its source and the end of a river is called its mouth. As the river water follows its path (course) from source to mouth, it carves out a channel (valley). Along a river's course there are different features and the shape of the valley changes. These variations are caused by the river, through processes known as erosion and deposition.

Erosion is the breaking up of the land (rocks, stones and earth). The force of a river's water erodes its banks. Rocks or stones carried by the river also erode the banks. The rocks and stones themselves break up into smaller pieces, as they collide with each other.

Deposition is the dropping of rocks, stones and silt by the river as it slows down.

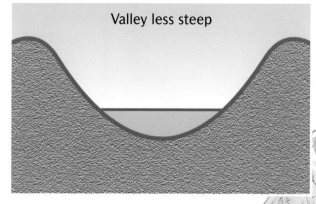

Valley less steep

delta

River Mouth
flat land (water very slow)
• deposition only

River Source
high ground
• excess rainwater

melting snow
and ice

springs

lakes

streams
drain into
channel

rapids   waterfalls

Upper Course
steep land (water flows fast)
• river transports
  boulders/stones
• lots of erosion

Middle Course
sloping land
(water flows a little slower)
• erosion
• river transports
  pebbles, sand, silt

tributaries
bring
more water

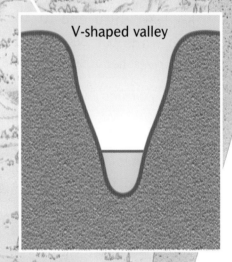

V-shaped valley

Lower Course
flat land (water slow)
• slow water deposits
  silt/sand
• less erosion

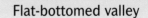

Flat-bottomed valley

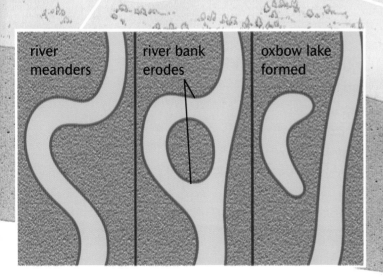

river
meanders

river bank
erodes

oxbow lake
formed

River research

Today we researched our local river to understand how it worked. Before we went to the river, Mr Bradley, our teacher, told us about a simple safety code because rivers can be dangerous places. This is the code:

> ## WARNING
> ◎ Never go near a river without an adult – stay within sight of the adult at all times.
> ◎ Do not paddle without being sure of the depth of water first.
> ◎ Do not go on slippery banks or banks that may be unstable.

Last week we looked on an Ordnance Survey map of our area and chose two different places along the river to visit. At one place the river is flat and bends slightly and at the other it goes down a hill. After we had discussed and made our decision, Mr Bradley had to get permission for us to work at the river because a farmer owned the land.

This morning, when we got to the river. Mr Bradley gave out notebooks, pencils, a cork, a fishing net and other instruments we would need. We split into two groups. My group headed for one part of the river and the other set off down the hill to the other.

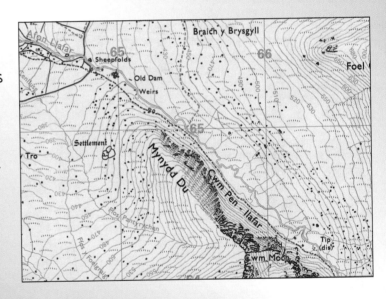

We used the Ordnance Survey map to find the right part of the river to measure. First of all we measured the velocity, which is another name for speed. I stood at a point beside the river and then my friend, Asif, measured a distance of 4m and stood there. Next I threw a cork in the river and then Asif shouted when it passed where he stood. Mr Bradley had a stopwatch and timed the cork from when it left me to when it passed Asif. We had to do this five times. I wrote down all the times that Mr Bradley had taken. Mel caught the cork in the fishing net each time so that we could use it again.

While we were doing this, the other group's task was to measure the gradient (the slope of the channel). They used a clinometer to do this.

Our next task was to find the size of the river and the depth. Mr Bradley photographed how we did it:

metre stick to measure depth of water/depth of channel

tape measure to measure width of water surface/width of channel

Finally, to find the size of the river's deposits, we picked up rocks and pebbles from the bank side and measured their diameter. Then we collected river water in a jar. We poured this through a fine strainer back into the river. There wasn't much left in the strainer, but Mr Bradley said Asif and I could weigh the silt we had collected when we got back to the classroom.

Back in the classroom, we worked out that our part of the river is upstream because it is on a steep gradient, had a steeper bank, lots of pebbles and was fast-flowing. Mr Bradley said that if it were in the middle it would also be moving quickly but would contain a lot of eroded silt and fewer pebbles. If it were further down stream it would be slower because there would have been more deposits of mud and silt and the bank side would not be so steep.

River investigation

You will need:

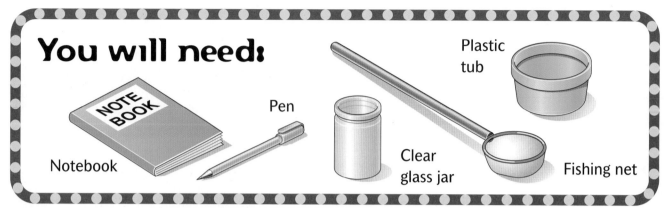

Notebook

Pen

Clear glass jar

Plastic tub

Fishing net

1 Draw two grids in the notebook and list the evidence to be gathered, as shown on the grids on page 43.

2 With an adult, choose an area of the river to research. There must be easy, safe access to the water, such as a firm bank which is not slippery. Check there is legal access to the river by asking the local landowner.

3 With an adult, take the necessary items to the selected river. Follow the Safety Code at all times. Use a stick to make sure the river edges are not too deep for safe paddling.

4 Inspect the river, recording all evidence on the grid.

a Scan the river for litter and other rubbish.

b Look for rainbow patterns of oil on the surface.

c Note whether any healthy-looking or dead/unhealthy-looking water animals or birds are present in the river or along the banks. Do not disturb any wildlife.

d Scoop water life from the river using the fishing net. Empty into the plastic tub with some water. Note if any clean-water insects/fish are present. Carefully return the sample to the river.

e Scoop a jar of water from the river. Note whether the water is cloudy or clear.

f Scoop mud from the bottom of the river using a fishing net. Note whether the mud smells bad or fresh.

g Use the fishing net to look for aquatic plants.

5 Leave the site and wash instruments and hands carefully.

6 Analyse the results to establish whether the river may be polluted.

7 If the river appears to be polluted, contact the Environment Agency.

Clean water insects

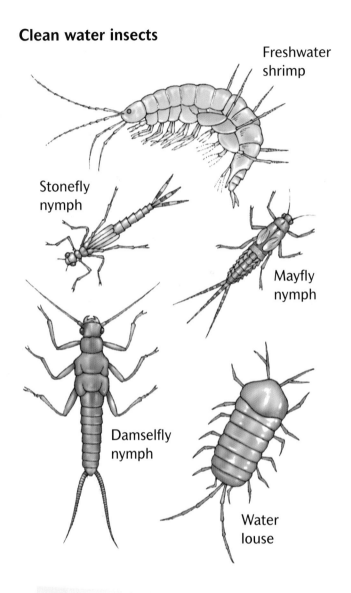

Freshwater shrimp

Stonefly nymph

Mayfly nymph

Damselfly nymph

Water louse

EVIDENCE OF POLLUTED WATER	✓
a Litter/rubbish	
b Oil on surface	
c No animals/birds found	
d Dead/unhealthy animals/birds found	
e No fish or clean-water insects	
f Cloudy water *	
g Foul-smelling mud	
h No aquatic plants	

EVIDENCE OF CLEAN WATER	✓
a No litter/rubbish	
b No oil on surface	
c Healthy animals/birds	
d Clean-water insects/fish	
e Clear water	
f Fresh-smelling mud	
g Aquatic plants	

* N.B. Cloudy water alone is not evidence of polluted water.

Glossary

altitude the height above sea level of an object or place

artificial fertilizers substances made from chemicals that are added to the soil to help plants grow. Artificial fertilizers include nitrogen and phosphate.

bore holes vertical holes, drilled into the earth to reach an underground water source

climate the main kinds of weather found in a place over a period of time

commercial farms farm where the farmers grow crops or keep animals for profit, rather than for their own needs

contaminated contaminated water contains pollutants, such as industrial wastes

discharge a substance released

droughts long periods in which there is very little or no rainfall

effluent liquid waste

fertilizer a substance that is added to the soil by farmers and gardeners to help plants grow

fresh water water from a natural source, such as a lake or a river, or from a reservoir

glaciers slow-moving masses of ice which usually begin high amongst mountains. The ice forms from many layers of snow

groundwater water held in rocks or soil underground

hydroelectric the process of creating power using falling water

ice-caps sheets of ice that cover the north and south polar regions of the Earth; a sheet of ice floats on the surface of the Arctic Ocean in the north and a dome-shaped sheet of ice covers much of the continent of Antarctica in the south

inhospitable very unwelcoming, where conditions are harsh

irrigation a system of watering plants, especially crops, such as a network of channels along which water is pumped

landfill sites large holes in the ground in which waste is dumped and buried

latitude the measurement of distance (in degrees) from the equator

mains water the main water supply that comes direct from where it is stored and purified

navigation directing a ship or boat down a river or on a route across the sea

pesticides chemicals used for killing pests, such as insects, that might otherwise ruin a crop

plumbing the pipes, tanks, drains and other fittings used for moving water and waste

pollutants   harmful substances, such as waste from dumps or industrial processes

precipitation   amount of rain and snow that has fallen

refugee camp   temporary home set up for people who have fled from their homes to escape from life-threatening problems, such as war and famine

reservoirs   artificial lakes that have been made for the storage of water

resource   a supply of something that is useful; natural resources include water, coal and oil

sewage   waste matter, for example the waste from toilets and drains

sewer   drainage pipe used for moving water or sewage away from a building

springs   a natural flow of water from out of the ground

ulcerated   having sores

water butt   barrel for collecting rainwater

Bibliography

Non-fiction

Bateman *The Oxford Children's A-Z Geography*
ISBN: 0 19 910086 1

Bowden *The Nile (A rivers journey)*
ISBN: 0750240415

Goodman *Earth in Danger: Rivers*
ISBN: 0750236205

Jennings *Geography Success Book 3* ISBN: 0 19 833845 7
and *4* ISBN: 0198338465

Jennings *The Oxford Children's A to Z of Science*
ISBN: 0 19 910992 3

Jennings *Natural Disasters series, Droughts*
ISBN: 1841387576

Langley *Oxford First Encyclopedia*
ISBN: 0 19 910804 8

Morgan *Oxford First Book of Science* ISBN: 0 19 910501 4

Parker *Pond and River* DK Eyewitness 1998
ISBN: 0863183182

Pollard *Great Rivers series, The Yangtze*
ISBN: 0237517183

Interface *Water* ISBN: 185434918X

The Young Oxford Encyclopedia of Science
ISBN: 0 19 910711 4

Fiction

Dickinson Elementals – *Water* 2002 David Fickling Books;
ISBN: 0385604580

Magorian *In deep water* 1994 Puffin Books
ISBN: 0140346732

Ransome *Swallows and Amazons* 1982 Jonathan Cape;
ISBN: 022460631X

Williamson *Tarka the Otter* 1995 Puffin Books
ISBN: 0140366210

Internet

www.internetgeography.co.uk/

www.bbc.co.uk/schools/landmarks/riversandcoasts/index.shtml

www.4learning.co.uk/essentials/geography/units/water_bi.shtml

www.thewaterpage.com

Organizations

The Environment Agency
Rio House, Waterside Drive, Aztec West,
Almondsbury,
Bristol
BS32 4UD
Phone: 08459 333111
http://www.environment-agency.gov.uk/kids/

Friends of the Earth
Friends of the Earth
26-28 Underwood Street
London
N1 7JQ
http://www.foe.co.uk/

Scottish Environment Protection Agency
SEPA Corporate Office
Erskine Court
Castle Business Park
Stirling
FK9 4TR
http://www.sepa.org.uk/education/water.htm

WaterAid, London
Prince Consort House
27-29 Albert Embankment
London
SE1 7UB
http://www.wateraid.org.uk

Water Companies

Thames Water www.waterinschools.com

Sutton and East Surrey Water
www.waterplc.com/WaterPlc/educat/educat1.html

Bristol Water www.bristolwater.co.uk/Education/

Yorkshire Water
www.yorkshirewater.com/yorkshirewater/main_edu.html

Anglia Water www.anglianwater.co.uk/

Welsh Water www.dwrcymru.co.uk/English/homepage.asp#

Water Service (Northern Ireland)
www.waterni.gov.uk/home1.htm

Scottish Water www.esw.co.uk/

South East Water www.southeastwater.co.uk/index.asp

United Utilties www.unitedutilities.com/

Index

Africa 9–10, 12, 14–15, 34–35
agriculture 21, 34, 36–37
aid agencies 10–11
air pressure 4, 8
Antarctica 8
Arctic 8
Aswan High Dam 34

bacteria 24
boats 11, 35
bore holes 8

cattle 12
China 18–19
chlorine 24
cholera 33
climate 8–9
clouds 5
crops 10–11, 14, 34, 36

dams 8, 18–19, 34
delta 34, 38
deposition 38–39
diseases 10, 14
drains 22–23
droughts 8, 10, 14, 31

ecosystems 19
Egypt 34–36
effluent 28
environment 18, 28
erosion 38, 39
Ethiopia 10

farmers 10, 34, 36–37
fertilizer 25, 28
fish 28
fishing 35
flood 11, 18–19

fluoride 25
fresh water 8, 10, 15, 24
Friends of the Earth 28–29

Ghana 12
glaciers 8
groundwater 28–29

hail 4
homes 11, 19–20, 25–27, 29, 32
humidity 8
hydroelectric power 18, 21

ice-caps 8
India 11
Industrial Revolution 32
industry 21, 25, 28, 34–35
insects 43
irrigation 18, 21, 34, 36

lakes 4–5, 8
landfill sites 29

mains water 22
meanders 39
monsoon 11

navigation 18
Nile 34–36

oceans 4, 8
OFWAT 29
organic food 29
Oxfam 14–15

pesticides 28–29
plumbing 22
pollution 18, 28–29
ponds 4
power 18, 19, 21, 25, 34

precipitation 9
purification 24, 31

rain 4, 7–8, 10, 30
rain gauge 6–7
rainfall 6, 8
reservoirs 19, 24–25
river code 43
river course 38–39
river investigation 42–43

sanitation 14
sewage 20–21, 24–25, 28, 31–33
sewage works 24–25, 28
sewer 23, 25, 33
shaduf 36–37
snow 4, 9, 39
springs 4, 8, 39
starvation 11, 14

temperature 4, 8–9
Three Gorges Dam 18–19
transport 11, 18, 21, 32, 35, 39

valley 38–39
Victorian times 32–33

Water Aid 14–15
water company 22, 29, 31
water cycle 4, 5, 25
water pump 15, 32
water vapour 4–5
weather 8–9
wells 8, 15–17, 32
well building 16–17
wildlife 19, 28–29, 42–43

Yangtze river 19